# My Life on Film

poems

## Helen Degen Cohen

Glass Lyre Press

Copyright © 2018 Helen Degen Cohen
Paperback ISBN: 978-1-941783-47-4

All rights reserved: except for the purpose of quoting brief passages for review, no part of this book may be reproduced or transmitted in any form or by any means, electronic or mechanical, including photocopying, recording, or by any information storage and retrieval system, without permission in writing from the publisher.

Cover art:  Helen Degen Cohen and Ruth Goring
Author photo:  Bill Yarrow
Design & layout: Steven Asmussen
Copyediting: Linda E. Kim

Glass Lyre Press, LLC
P.O. Box 2693
Glenview, IL 60025
www.GlassLyrePress.com

# Contents

## Wand

| | |
|---|---|
| River Upon Which | 3 |
| Zhang Yimou: *To Live* | 4 |
| Shadows | 7 |
| Putting the Flying Saucers in the Wash | 8 |
| To the Circus Lady in *Wings of Desire* | 10 |
| Young Men of Rimini | 11 |
| Earrings in Tajikistan | 12 |
| It's Cinematography, Love | 14 |
| Dance of the Muses | 16 |
| Life on Film | 19 |
| The Holy Poem | 21 |

## Woman

| | |
|---|---|
| Gong Li | 25 |
| Seventeen-Year Cicadas | 27 |
| First leaf, | 29 |
| Not That the Life of a Saint | 32 |
| Her Man | 33 |
| White Heron | 34 |
| *Women in Love* | 36 |
| *Maborosi* | 38 |
| Her C | 40 |
| *Ponette* | 41 |

## Woman (cont'd)

| | |
|---|---|
| Said— | 43 |
| Gradisca | 44 |
| *Hush little baby, don't say a word* | 45 |
| This Bitter Earth | 47 |
| Ozu Moment | 48 |
| Au Revoir, Belmondo | 49 |
| *House of Pleasures* | 50 |

## Salò

| | |
|---|---|
| *Salò* | 55 |
| *L'Argent* | 57 |
| *Mishima* | 59 |
| *Breathless* | 60 |
| Childhood | 61 |
| good evening, mr. wallenberg | 62 |
| Dear pale blue film | 63 |
| We Are Starlets | 66 |
| The Hours Are Sad | 68 |
| "The tunnel at the end of the light" | 69 |
| Litany with lines from Paradjanov and Bresson | 70 |
| *The Russian Ark* | 71 |

## Space

| | |
|---|---|
| That Which Gives Us Life | 76 |
| "Hitchcock loved silence" | 77 |
| *Gabbeh* | 80 |
| In the Dark | 82 |
| Faint | 83 |
| To a Child | 85 |
| The sets are awash with our leaving | 86 |
| On Landscape | 87 |
| *She replied,* | 90 |
| We | 91 |
| *Immortal beloved,* | 92 |
| Touch | 93 |
| | |
| Acknowledgments | 97 |
| About the Author | 99 |

# WAND

*It's sad, having to go to sleep;
you're forced to part.*
—"Patricia Franchini" in *Breathless*

# River Upon Which

I float my love of film
as if love were containable only
in water, and film too—
my love of our lost faces,
our Bogarts and Bacalls, our Annes,
Jacks and Johns, Bettys and Bettes,
shallows in blue. Preserved
in river water, clear and undying.
And somehow, they on film,
and they who only died, merge—
they on film raise up the others like
grounded stars into their never
dissolving photos, and hold them,
while all we remember distinctly
was surely once on film. My love is
aqua-green, my love is blue, my love
is a flowing sun, is sheer. Amber
strikes it yellow, it shrieks—Robert
Mitchum in *The Night of the Hunter,*
two small children believing—for evil
floats on film as beautifully as anything,
though a teacher in *The Miracle Worker*
can calm even a speechless child
held close, until it is safe—or we can
sail the numbed skies in *Brazil*, or join
the woman in *Raise the Red Lantern,*
stalking herself in a cage so lovely
it saves her from giving in. Oh afloat,
all, and deep, and beside the river
I can see us singing of air and fire,
earth and movement, of moving
pictures while other pictures
are imprisoned—an insomnia of pictures.

# Zhang Yimou: *To Live*

1. Film

First, before any character
begins to grow into us,
before any regime makes our friends
enemies, even before hunger
or thirst, there is color (the blue
of war comes later): a prism, street
of people—walls, hats and baskets, voices
sharp as old trees, bicycles, sky—
red, dream-orange and blue. The colors
in the house hush to talk; outside, air;
whatever else may happen, we breathe
color—yet within the color someone always
has to rise to the brutish call of
another, get dressed, do
the impossible or the indistinct,
Liberation!, like a noise of alien cymbals
crashing, a call to the closing of doors,
smiling and bowing deeper.
Once again sweat enriches
the pavement, walls, skin—laborers
melt into their own frieze.


2. To Live

Morning rises over Zhang Yimou
blue and golden. He has given
life to morning, his eyes
awash in ordinary mourning:
beautiful faces, golden and blue,
used like so much cloth by history,
like so much dye, leaf, root
and wine. The powerful are drunk
for a moment, then die, then others

are drunk for a moment. Gong Li
dresses for the part. Being woman
she turns blue and golden, perhaps a bird,
a thing for the runners of things,
her body of sweat and lucent paleness
disintegrates back to history.


3. The Puppet Opera

The puppet opera comes from nowhere
into the film,
which is why it is holy.
And because no one knows it.
Does Zhang Yimou know, or is he,
too, holy? No,
it is his eye that knows, a witness,
a sometimes acquaintance:
the cut-out puppets so delicate, so limited,
one sees through them, one sees
the hand that moves them, the shrill mouths
that sing: the eccentric singing
blooms louder than the sun, and everyone
laughs and cheers. The puppets:
a man and woman. The puppets:
soldiers killing soldiers,
tossing them into a heap.
Handcrafted by no one.
Sung with everything a man possesses,
by no one. The voices belong to no one.
And Zhang Yimou is no one.
But the puppet theater come from nothing
golden, says Zhang Yimou,
the word brash blue.

4. China

Morning rises on Zhang Yimou
but in China it is only China rising
on a bicycle coming from over the horizon,
her rags burning, her two infants
hung asleep, her barefoot husband
running behind, waving frantically
at Zhang Yimou, who paints them
blue and golden, golden and blue.

# Shadows

*after Shadows of Our Forgotten Ancestors*

Dolls run through the forest,
the spellbinding trees.
No, the trees are snowed in,
their sap unmuttering.
But no, they have no sap at all
and the mountain is cold and white.

Dolls, in red-and-green socks,
we run for each other as if joy
could outrun all the white,
as if throats, repeating, repeating,
could draw magic out of our dead—
who also sang, once, only brasher,
louder across the slopes; such tall trees
and one fell on my brother—

Oh
Marichka, Marichka, where are you,
first my brother and now
you too, buried and lamented,
our kin in their best woolens,
singing, echoing, deafening, choirs
rough as bark. Oh Marichka,
I knew you as a child, we were lovers
long, long before time, before
the water swallowed you up,
and so I will lie down on the water.

Marichka, you are the wind-in-the-trees
that is music
outside the cold,
and also inside
our warm patterns,
our great white tunics
and furs, inside

where we sing. *We will be together,* we sing.
*We will never be together,* we sing.

# Putting the Flying Saucers in the Wash

This is not about the movies
but the makers.
How they wiped their hands on
a clean sheet hung out in the sun,
how they had to endure the clean sheet,
an entire house of clean sheets
and gleaming floors, the little
toy soldiers lined up in the child's room,
the ground beneath them dusted daily,
and the new saucers in place,
everything new, no robes but
in the closet, no comfort but in
price—
                        she'd wiped
her leaf-stained hand on that
white sheet in the sun and it cost
a hundred dollars, she was told
by a very disappointed hostess—
                        *this is my house.*
And it was. And they had to
endure the guilt and the organized
floor they stepped on, the fresh
cleaned words in the conversation
about food and war—the war
extra fresh-cleaned—and the children
in college or married or unmarried,
all with hundred dollar sheets
hung in the sun by the part-time
maid who was herself spotless,
her time organized in half, the
other half dark, so dark

they wanted to make a movie of it
and they brought in the cameras,
all the lovely chaos, images
and dreams.

And the dreams blew everything
asunder and down came the clean sheets
off the line, and the new cups
from England
couldn't be found except
for the one touching the happy
maker's lips.

# To the Circus Lady in *Wings of Desire*

I tell this lie:

There's always a troupe on Sundays,
the tulips blaze, even the fireflies turn
into dancers, the little
theater company turns up
      and the elephants waltz.

      So one day I asked if I could join them,
      growing heavy with want.
      They saw my weight,
      they saw me trumpeting.
      I couldn't help being the honest animal
      I was, my feet stone blocks.
      Sometimes all I want to do
      is feather my way through the bulk
      and this is when the scale tips
      for real.
           Pray for mercy, girl.
           You were fired before you were hired.
           Yet somehow, Sunday remained Sunday.
           Then the troupe folded up & went home.
           The little theater, the dancers,
the gypsies in bright yellow
skirts, the music man,
the circus girl in *Wings of Desire,* all the writers
in the world named Kafka or Rilke
or William Butler Yeats, knife swallowers
and hoops of fire, and the little
girl in the corner, twirling out of sight.

# Young Men of Rimini
### on revisiting *Amarcord*

It wasn't the snow that
fell in feathery drifts, or
the white puffballs of spring
"snowing" dreamlike,
or the real peacock opening like
a vision, above, or the great
ship of lights from another world,
········it was just that
one of the boys (nearly men now)
began moving, very slowly,
in front of the building, to an
imperceptible rhythm in the
weather, that sudden wind; it was
dark now and flakes blew across
like fragments of someone's
soul flavoring the weather,
the way a bowl of apples can
flavor the air with a whole galaxy
of orchards and warm
afternoons.
········It was just that
one of the boys (almost men)
began moving with the ease
of a snowflake, to whatever
light illuminates snowflakes in
the dark.
········His movements
grew slowly, the wind urging him on,
he moved his shoulders
(hands in pockets), his torso,
and finally his feet, and
the others—as though they had
just caught the pleasant malady,
moved as well, but slowly,
because there was no other
kind of time in the world
but cinema.

# Earrings in Tajikistan
### after Mohsen Makhmalbaf's *The Silence*

I peeked out a window in Europe.
So many cherries in the orchard!
For sure! Many, many cherries.
Thousands. Cherries
are better than angels,
cherries drip if you're lucky

and some were just beginning to color—

two or three or four on a stem
so many, a pretty cherry tree—

a pretty cherry berry cherry tree!

In a town the color of ice cream

the girl carefully adjusts her
fresh cherry earrings, a twin stem over

each ear, head dancing to music
from afar . . . even as blind little Khorshid

loses his way following the joy-beat
of the street musician—but suddenly
he is missing too long! and
the girl with the cherry earrings

runs—we've lost her, but here now is
the street musician again
boarding a bus, jamming away nonstop,
the blind boy after him—we
are on the bus with the rollicking

music—surely we must know the boy

will be found, even as our bodies sway
with worry, our quarter minds

tap-tap to the music—
as somewhere the girl with cherry earrings

runs!—
even as the camera

has *already* found him—oh

oh, there must have been
so many cherries, thousands and
thousands of cherries in the orchard.

# It's Cinematography, Love

> *I've heard there's a kind of bird with no legs.*
> *All it can do is fly and fly. When it gets tired*
> *it sleeps on the wind. The bird can only land once*
> *in its whole life. That's the moment he dies.*
> —Days of Being Wild, directed by Wong Kar-wai

that flies
not the legless bird who must never land
his bleached heart trailing
into the future
or is it a train ride
in darkly saturated green
edges and angles cutting through with
methyl-green sharp knives
or is it a train ride
into the sugar-rush,
America's 50s done up Asian
with a Latin beat
the way the world mixes it up
now that we have this common language
and it's the cinematography
of abandonment, a screen
nine-tenths dark, a nearblindness or is it a man
thinking himself a bird
cutting through the shades
of women who want. Calamine
blue gliding through
irony like a sexy song, call it
*capturing*—the available light
in their eyes and it's
called *Days of Being Wild,*
as time tapers to its end like a solitary
witness to such
women's eyes, and his, the indifferent
bastard we love.
And it's cinematography
in pale brown, his full mouth
waiting for her throat to come to *him,*
the flick of her bared
shoulder and the light unquivering.

It's the back of him dancing
the fuck-you
mambo to the mother
who abandoned him
in green moonlight, it's
cinematography
that flies, not
the bird who's been dead
all along, so we're told
in that story about how he just
had to keep flying.

# Dance of the Muses

Bresson on *A Man Escaped*—a semi-cento

—and dizzy with recovery from that bug,
the cinematic *out there* nods off the screen, he says

*Speaking makes us think*

its logic clogging the thickest pond
a frog ever had to negotiate—

*The impossibility of communication*
*is the basis of all my work*

and he quotes Degas's orange and blue
way of seeing hands on a ballet shoe—Degas, who said

*The muses never speak to each*
*other. They only dance together*
*sometimes.*

In the window's *out there,* trees every inch pregnant
with one or another green—

*I'll never manage to do it all*
*before I die*

green tangling faster than growth, my eyes
tangled in green—

*order creates*
*chaos gives life*

—and I owe him this, and the others too, I who
escape into dark ground like a seed—

*I try to show only certain parts*
*and hint at the rest*

or into the shadow of a leaf which stands
for tree—no, says he

*portray nature using nature,*
*but don't copy it*

Good God. I remember only that I woke up suddenly
to nothing, no light in the shift or drift—

*It's in the joints and cracks*
*that poetry and nature are found*

—eyes dragged open; world filling in
the window. And still he is talking—

*We don't see what we think we see*
*What we see isn't what the camera sees*

Get me a camera, higher power, I hallucinate,
to touch even one of their countless faces—

*The Passion of Joan of Arc*

on his and everyone's lips—Dreyer's film in which he
lifts her face onto the screen and says: *live!*

*Yes . . . the film brings the characters to life*
*and not vice versa*

This I believe. This. That other things than this
can happen. The opposite.

*The supernatural is natural*

That the odor of grass is *in* the room, not out there,
its green wine going to my head. He cautions:

*Poets don't denature nature*

Out there a man was trying to escape.
A woman was captured and sentenced to death.

Her face opens clean as a lion's. Smoke rises in the sky, holy above the byre. And Bresson.

*I'm simply trying to paint.*

# Life on Film

My life on earth was all matter.
My life on film is everything
that has ever floated through me
condensed to a cloud I can recline on,
not a thing for worms.
                      My life
on film remains buoyed
by a song-and-dance man,
an orchestra slowing the approach of a small house
on a mountain,
                  is a life
hurt to pieces then pasted together again,
plotless, defying definition.
                  My life on film is
often beautifully defined:

If you were still here, love,
we might make us a beautiful remake, our anger
thrashing against some Annie Sullivan
who would lead us to water, if only
we could shape the meaning of water, give words to our
signing, invent new definitions—"you"
might be the river in the film *Poetry*
that runs patiently beyond
our life on earth, but never beyond
                  our life on film.

But if you were still here, love,
how would I recognize my life on film—

where you might be reduced
to a gesture—as in an old video clip, our decades of hair reversing
from gray to brown. In my life on film
                                I'm redone
into every color I've been, every age, every flutter, like the one
before you said, "Would you like to dance?"—

      —redone into every wish, every gender . . .
        like that villager in the film *Ugetsu*:

*I row for everyone, between two equally strange worlds*

      —or perhaps a blonde
cool as Ingrid.

In my life on film, which depends on some prior life,
I am busy for all our sakes—commissioned,
reeling—no. My life on earth
was all matter. In my life on film I
float just above you (look up)
and descend

into your heart—every woman I've ever been—
descend into your brawny chest where you promised
to keep us safe

if only you weren't such an idiot
in your life on earth—

until we've both turned transparent and
others can walk through us
at this wide-lens moment, love,

and we walk through them.

# The Holy Poem

Those who say this is wrong—tough,
we're going to the movies with God
who goes daily and smokes a tinted cigar.
(She may be a goddess.)
Those who say "we are blessed"
may never know when they're cursed,
can never say "we are fortunate,"
their language half-blessed.

*For we are everything, everyone.*

How many ways does a god walk?
We all begin barefoot.
We are all frightened and amazed and
open the movie-house doors with a cry.

*And out of this, I will make everything.*

I came, I conquered.
I curled up safe in a gorilla's hand.
I let my skirt fly in the wind.
I taught a little girl how to talk
with her hands. She said, "Water."

*And we walked on water.*

It was an evening for all the gods in the world.

# WOMAN

*. . . and if my life
is like the dust
that hides, mmm, the glow
of a rose
what good am I
heaven only knows.*

—from "This Bitter Earth,"
sung by Dinah Washington in *Killer of Sleep*

# Gong Li

    for the actress in *Raise the Red Lantern*

Some faces should never speak
but remain carved and polished not in
porcelain but a creamy alabaster
set with small moist gems (nose, eyes, mouth)
in a dignified moon-face atop
a gown in Chinese-sky-blue silk.

But if required to speak
make the language moan atonal
make it squeak, make the opera rub the wrong way
like chalk, so we know the strangeness
that emerges out of skin-soft not-porcelain
is human error.

Let the beauties agree. Let the four moon-faces
hang suspicious, the bud-mouths contort over
whom the master will favor tonight, which wife
gets the royal foot massage—with mallets.

Let the moons keep their secrets, though
a belly pops now and then and the master must be assured
of sons. Let silken robes get undone, sheer
mauve curtains enclose the favorite—wife Number Four—
queened for the night, the red lantern hung
over her door, a lucent, red-orange moon.

Let the real moon go palely incidental, absent.
Let whatever is natural be man-made, elegantly
formal, though (some suggest)

brutal with history. Rumor has it that some wife
of not-so-long-ago was muffled or perhaps
hung, for the world's most infamous misdemeanor: adultery;
and no breathing wife has the bad sense
—or insanity—to play detective or

does she?

All moons set
but the moon blue loveliest
in unkempt exquisite
circles the well
circles the well

*circles the well in the courtyard*
      *as sweet wife Number Five makes her entrance*
circles the well hair
of reason being
a matter of free
will circle the well
will deep the well of
circles tall very tall
being wisps of hair
matter being
tall of circles wild
will of the matter
being being
free of and then
a history of the moon
stray haired in exquisite
silken secret pattern
matter handpicked
round the well
gorgeous moon number
four Chinese
she

because the mad
are not to be
undisturbed

# Seventeen-Year Cicadas

while under the influence of the documentary
*The Spider, the Mistress, and the Tangerine*
*(the life and work of Louise Bourgeois)*

Red. Red eyes of my mother, on me.
Of glass, moist as cherry. Bright

      (red).

Wings swooped back.
      Head of hard mud.
Red veins fanning back and up into foggy
      webs, tucked neatly
          (back)
      into foggier, translucent webs. Wings.

Red tentacle stilts out front, to prop on
a mussel-head resting on delicate claw-end
      legs propped up
her face and the eye on me.

Red veins, folded back into cathedral
      wings, translucent, hiding
      the black body
          (black),      demure,
      within the lovely, updrifting curtain of
      stained glass wing-meeting-wing
      like hands in prayer. Translucent hands.
        (Red veins pulsing.)
        (Red eye.) Of pretty lady.
Eyeing me. Behind her a leaf's cushiony
green. Solid leaf green.

Lady, let me appear thus
every seventeen years,
my gown palatial, my gossamer gown all
      red stays
   on succulent green,

    reclining on my tummy elbow-up
my two gigantic red-ball eyes

looking aslant at the irrelevant giant
with her thingamajig
that flashes
with so much uncertainty,

        the glass bead of my eye
        finding her too big a cloud to bother
        with. She is world,

whatever that means. And I,
a red-veined lady on a leaf,
I'm at ease for the longest moment
there is.

In the dark, she's the after-image
of a jewel.

# First Leaf,

yellow-veined throughout the red—
when I first picked you up
I was thinking of Nobody,
    the half-Indian
in *Dead Man* with Johnny
Depp, that black-and-white flick
by Jarmusch in which
    death is much foretold
among trees so photographic
they almost make you bleed.

But this is all a lie.
What I really was thinking of
was a child no longer a child
(first my oldest, then my youngest
then the one in the middle)
and worrying about each by
turns, just as all you leaves
    were turning, everywhere—

except in *Dead Man*
(and you are my first
leaf of the season) last night,
like an apparition.

My children (William
Blake, accountant, trapped
in the Wild West, dreams
of color in a world made black
and white) and now you
half-burning with color
    in my hand.

And to tell you the truth,
I don't know what to
    make of it. The term was
    *glazing*, in the old

painting days, it meant
one fine, almost spiritual, layer
superimposed on another,
   on a child's eyes, as if
     bleeding through the
       surface of a town
soaked in the afterlight

      of a storm—last night

on the screen, barely covering
an ancient hell-hole in the West
    minus purple-mountained
           majesties.

*On this side of the river,*
                says Nobody,
*you'll have to speak through your gun,*
     *William Blake,*
      *accountant,*
and long and long and long
     is death,
taking up the entire movie.

          Leaf,
   three maple wings
  flushing at the thought,
your red and green denying everything,
   as would my three winged
        children—
  not a thought to any of this

slow thinking that oozes
color by the minute.

So I put you on the desk,
across a lined notepad,
growing a sudden hunger
    for paint.
(At the end, a radiant black-and-white
      cloud takes forever to fade
            in William's eyes.)
                  Leaf,
I will make you bleed eternally.

# Not That the Life of a Saint

can be measured in days or seconds
but that Brigit can kiss a dog's face
when he walks and talks that way.
                                    Not that saints
are better than we are, but that Brigit
can fall to her knees while others
fall into old conversations over
done best, gone sick, or good sport
and Brigit gets up not from the floor
but from fields of orange flowers in the
                                    floorboards.
Not that saints don't mind dying, only that
Brigit can sing straight through a funeral.
The day is marrow-dark.
The lights are yellow.
Not that the saints fall prostrate before
a gilded annunciation or a stone Mary,
only that Brigit is deaf and dumb since birth,
and it's only that Brigit can see eleven
worlds on a canvas, her brush dripping
what others would call blood—
Brigit, who doesn't understand suffering,

Lord, may all her days come true.

Or as we said back home, it's dawn,

let us yoke the oxen and wake the cows
and seed the hard dirt with gold.

# Her Man

    after the subject of *Modigliani*

Andy Garcia has stolen your smile,
has carried it straight from the moon
into my body, where it spreads and
weakens my bones.
I look away
                        but I want to know
what happens to the woman with
the bellyful of child? What
in the world will she do
                without him?
He smiles, oh God. And like all the others I—
but I want to know, will he stay
this time? Will he drink himself
to death? Or leave some
other way? How many ways are there
to leave a woman who can never leave
                a man who paints
her long, beautiful neck and diamond-blue
                eyes?
Picasso has applauded—now the world knows
he'll be famous
                but out in the street, it is not Amedeo,
this staggering man again, beaten up and
                dying by moonlight—it is
                the *boy*
who has always shadowed the man, as he does even now
        sitting so alive on the cold pavement
            beside the man

        *the child you were, Modi*

blithely sweeping the inhuman blue snow
                        through your fingers

# White Heron
   after Wong Kar-Wai's *2046*

*No one ever returns from 2046.*

All those genuine loves,
woman after woman,
were color, in room 2046, were
color and lush music, steeped ever
deeper, their love turned to
jeweled colors of the
core, the two or three
colors of fire, their desire
spilling eyes into prisms
and stains.
        *Siboney...*
              sang the odor
of hot satin and lip, Latin melodies
for hearts on fire, never doused,
nor the cool sides of fire, changing
nothing.

*Not even in some city in the future, in digital space.*

*I don't know you,*
she might have said, *you
with slicked hair and tie,* but was,
of course,
too beautiful to say it, Hong Kong woman
in saturated color. *You are so kind to me,*
she said instead. Sparkling,
lipsticked. And he heated up every hue
for her, in whatever casino, in a dark
street, perhaps even

*but this is impossible, it is not in the film*

in our own woods
across the river where
a white heron
stands timeless and still,
forever at peace
as if in some other life—then suddenly
spreads its wings and vanishes.
Into what?

These are not images from the movie,
all of which (you may not like this)
have gone white with the
white heron.

*No one ever returns from 2046.*

# Women in Love

The meaning of cold:
a brawny, breathing, accomplished enemy
who will injure, will emerge
out of the white, not blue, out of
pictures etched on an icy sky—
Glenda Jackson
has been studying the color.

How tall must she be
to get it right? How familiar with
the nature of this sky? Especially the most hidden heat
would be lethal. Gudrin, her character,
must be warmed with cold,

and Gerald now, for wanting Gudrin, must approach
slowly—just as *she* must approach
the horned buffalo. Still, a horse beater is more than
the horse's equal. Hot blood
moves Gerald, yet how
is one to be moved? to be warmed?

Gudrin's sister, that little heater,
walks beside her, practically causing
things to grow. Perhaps a shorter woman
is closer to growing things. One can just
feel her loving and dying. Growing and wilting.
A flower of a sister—who loves Birkin
the questioner, who loves to wrestle
Gerald. And so the magnetic twist,
as if opposites could ever attract.

But this is about cold.
About an oak, not a flower, an animal-tree
rooted in knowledge, not dirt, in outcomes like
one and one equals one, as in love that wants
and love that uses. It is all (all *what*, says tall Gudrin)
about man-on-man questions writhing

in naked chests—virile feathers and furs—
the difference between cold men and cold
women and which one

will walk the distance
into the heart of snow

# Maborosi
   (the quietest movie in the world)

A story of stills      modestly lit
and in every frame                              eventually
a movement
                    a darkness on two feet
a girl-woman with hair tied back
entering into    coming out of    distance    like a spell—

tandem bicycle in happy city     shared room—

              profile
hands, one worrying the other
(same street   same train    tracks     street tracks
the waiting)—
square of light      doorway?

pencil of light      lengthening
    shortening
   waiting    long foyers of waiting
quiet with happening (cool piano)—
                              train voyage: interior.

~~

Narrow frame: sea-light far
off: a figure    two figures?    (wind)
along a thin line    ordinary shoreline    as in
*your* world, one of the thousand stills
in which you move your overburdening
*why* locked in the—

formal aperture     door or window
           where movement is
painstakingly slow . . .      like a fact you can't quite take in
                              *the new man, patient*—

Then you know: it is loss, so simple
it teeters.

     Sounds
           of children
playing     the sea        and again

     out of sea-calm
                   the call of the children.

House or porch.
Two seated figures, staring out to sea
     darkness like an angel     in which thoughts tendril     tendril
       then one voice thinks to remark on
the new spring warmth in the air

     then more silence

         footage     long as life

# Her C

    for Bela Tarr's *Sátántangó*

If you leave her crotch in the movie it may not be
a big deal; it may even shine, to some. But
have her washing it down, for more than two
minutes and—it's crucified. Our existence is
good, our effort to exist, disgusting.

We want the product not the piss.
Not the goopy makeup but the doll.
Not the workout but the score and
by how much—that bit of an inch that brings out the stars.
Not your doggy foraging, or what you found in the ditch,
but how close you got to being the grownup they
wanted you to be, their car music, their showtime.

Bela Tarr put her crotch in the movie at some
distance, so you could finish your meat. But
Jesus, she's *washing it down,* fat as the world's flab,
squatting over a bucket, and you thought
white lilacs for your bride, and all those stars
long stared out of sight, splattered by the time
you saw them, or you wouldn't be had.

Don't even whisper what it takes to make it
through life and how it all turns out. Switch
channels for half of that *Sátántangó* shit, you,
in the mud like a half-dead cat that wouldn't know
an angel from a fishsteak, your eyes tired with seeing,
lungs tired with breathing, your ass long overdue for
a bucket of hot water and soap. Ah . . . that's
better. Get on with it and
a beer, because her C is hot with
what life is about.

# Ponette

A small, reasonable child in France
has no right to lose her mother:
mother the sun is gone but still
the child must play, the children
kiss and are kind to the child and still
she has too many questions—the sky
has its rules and everyone mentions God
and Jesus and the heaven where mothers
go and are happy, and still when
the light is behind the earth—the child
listens.
                *Speak to me, mother.*
I have prayed, as I was instructed,
I have gone through four trials, I have
followed others, leapt fearfully, climbed into the dark
and slept, but—woke up listening when
                *sometimes you came to me*
though not everyone believed it—and then
your voice rolled out of reach. I am not
cold though they say it's cold
today, I am *here*.

*Speak to me, vanished mother.*

*Mother, you must speak!*

The schoolyard opens, releasing children.
They perch and fly by like the birds.
*A child is more powerful than a mother,*
        *mother, come to me, mother!*

What can a mother do but promise?

And on the appointed day, she came, for a picnic, a long
long walk through mild meadows and woods, to just
have a good time, laugh, and promise

that she never went away
and never will.
And so goodbyes are
simple.

The father, just arrived in town, listens, as if to a long
lost letter in his hand.

# Said—

Said Imamura, her hands are spiders.
Said Mizokuchi, a wife, begotten of grace and myth.
Said Oshima, she is as disgusting as anyone.
Said Ozu, she is composed.

Said Imamura, she climbs the year bravely.
Said Oshima, she wants men.
Said Mizoguchi, she waves goodbye to a stranger in the mist.
Said Ozu, she is tall and slender.

Said Mizoguchi, the stranger was once her husband.
Said Ozu, it is not you, mother, it is Tokyo.
Said Imamura, his hunger is impoverished beside her hunger.
Said Oshima, she is body.

Said Ozu, sister, is it you among the graceful verticals.
Said Oshima, notice the puking, used-up young.
Said Imamura, her blistering hands at the shuttle.
Said Mizoguchi, time passes.

Said Imamura, she is dense as earth.
Said Mizoguchi, she is the other woman—she is death.
Said Ozu, she kneels beside her father's sandals.
Said Oshima, she is Japan.

# Gradisca

    for all the characters in the film

*Amarcord*, my mad love, my
childhood that has nothing
to do with smallness

my spiraling spectacle of
everything proudly grotesque—
she in her bold red hair, your grand

Rimini *bambolina* sashaying
her ample red satin rump
to Mussolini's military beat—

varoom, varoom, varoom
go Italy's loose parts
steady as a slow hot pendulum

we're hoping to catch up with—
even as the stupid *fascisti* disappear
into their uniforms and *we* are growing

into men, slow-dancing with stars
in our eyes, as white puffballs
float down to a hypnotized earth

and the now famous peacock spreads
his wings on top of—what was it?—
up high in the mist—

and we freeze
between *that* and
Gradisca's lovely glove touching

her white fur collar,
an adorable sound escaping her red lip-
sticked, wide-screen smile.

# Hush little baby, don't say a word

for Anne Bancroft and Patty Duke in *The Miracle Worker*

*Mama's gonna buy you a mockingbird*

And the speechless, hearingless, blind child
feels a monstrous storm calming, falling
to its knees. She stuffs the calm like meat
in her teeth, it goes down like a cloud
gone wee and pink, if the child could say pink

*And if that mockingbird don't sing*

In the morning the creature itself is a storm,
is all thunder and wild winds that can do
nothing but crash into walls, knees and elbows,
costly china, and, hardest to understand, love

*And if that looking glass gets broke*

This thing, this song the other sings
wraps around her, she is terrified of new
promises, the storm itself shattered, even
the shards gone, strange thirst unquenched

IT HAS A NAME, child, taste it! (straight from
the well, it flows, it falls, it fills your hands wet—)

*And if that cart and bull turn over*

These questions tormenting the other
(what if you never hear me)

*And if that dog named rover won't bark*

(and what if I lose this game)

*And if that horse and cart fall down*

*Wah-er,* says the child, and poets wake from their thirst
every living creature wakes, *water*

rings loud and clear, coming from
their own kind, as if everything they see,

hear

or utter were their own water-hearts breaking
open,
every tree, lake, lip and cheekbone, nose

and hurricane—calming to the warm tide
of the others' arms around the one. *Yes*, they agree,

*it has a name.* It, too, has a name.

# This Bitter Earth

Now the dance scene in *Killer of Sheep,*
between husband and wife, about
two minutes long (every moment
of the film is a life), and I am the woman
reaching for my man, reaching slowly,
first for the nearest part of him, chest,
then arm, shoulder, then back
smooth as a mountain, its breeze
wrapping round me, and I can feel
the mountain trying to respond, yes
it wants to respond, but if ever a
mountain had shining muscular arms
to put around anyone, they're tired,
tired, run down, bulldozed smooth as
steel on a coffee pot, hot and helpless
and still full of love.
            *This bitter earth,*
sings Dinah Washington because she
knows, *what fruit it bears / what good
is love, mm* (Dinah's pauses are lives)
*that no one shares—ooh, ooh,* sings Dinah,
and every *ooh* is a life, every breath,
and closer still, each molecule of inhaled
air, each atom of barely sustainable
atmosphere—a life. *And if my life /
is like the dust, / oooh, that hides /
the glow of a rose / what good am I /
heaven only knows.*
            *This bitter earth,*
sings Dinah, and regardless
of how it goes, we are dancing.
And the earth grows bigger, one remembers
a bright blue ball spinning in dark space,
unconscious, or as some claim, serene,
blithely autonomous, detached, at peace.
The way Kubrick must have seen it
on a bright blue night in spring,
earth's moment as an odyssey from
life to life to life,
            this bitter earth.

# Ozu Moment

Sadness begins with
the bond between parent and child.

Long silence and finally words
like wounds. *I would like us
to live together but . . .*
Words inadequate to loneliness,
therefore silence. Statues
of living flesh, the work of
mute artists.

A train goes by.

Cityscapes solid in the wind, wash lines.
The crowds speak for no one
but everyone speaks for the crowds.
Real bonds never disentangle.
The factory next door makes too much noise
for sleeping, and silence is too loud a lullaby.

It is not my fault, mother, that I haven't
succeeded. It is Tokyo.
It is not my fault that you sacrificed for me,
not my fault that you are
a good mother.

A train goes by.

The room holds its breath.

# Au Revoir, Belmondo

    after *Breathless*

But    if not for the cigarette dangling
from those *lips*
you would not be you (faux Bogie)

your swagger, your unconcern with
this movie you're in,
or anything    other than sweet Jean
in her polka-dots,

your pristine American cutie
with her equal cigarette, in her now
pert little *striped* dress, little boy's haircut,
little things that will be the
death of you,

smoking skinny Belmondo folding into
yet another hot car off the street,
running your finger along your
    thick *lips*
    as if suddenly something mattered—
even if not to us, *mon ami,*
who want so much more than you do
to try and sleep soundly—

Jean-Paul—just like
that girl selling dailies
on the avenues and wondering,
like a plucked daisy, whether
she does, or doesn't —love you,

even when you've caught
the bullet and lain down
    like a good boy
in the middle of the final street.
She brushes *her* finger
    across *her* lips.

# House of Pleasures
   *after the French period film*

We were not born sisters.
Nor were we taught to use simple language, here.
Yet here we are in these red,
                mirrored rooms, pleasing.
Men rule the world more than ever.
Yet up in the little salons and down
in the big one, we, our masks
warm as wine for so long now,
having lived within the same walls
that keep us from the world
in sickness and in health,
sometimes laughing, sometimes singing,
sometimes dying of the clap,
we are sisters.

Will you dance with me?
Your painted cheeks so pretty,
your sweat washed so clean.
I remember teaching you how to do it,
where to put the fragrance,
what to show first and do last.
How to live with your face gashed.
There are no gangsters here, only
gentlemen with knives.
When the house closes
we will be in the streets.

In that new century, where will you be?
Your perspiration is still mine.
My undergarments fit you.
We had almost the same mother.
We kiss with the same lips,
the doors are still locked, all of them.
Your flesh is still warm.

*If we don't burn, how will we light up the night?*

Before you forget me, will you dance with me
one more time? Sweet, and only with me,
love, dear sister? Hold me. If you die,
the house will go dark.

# Salò

*An artist, if he's unselfish and passionate,
is always a living protest.*
—Pier Paulo Pasolini

*The only performance that matters, that really matters, that makes it all worthwhile, is madness.*

—Mick Jagger in *Performance*

*. . . I made a film that pleased the audience, so I hope the second film will displease hugely and that it will inspire me to make films again. That's what it is, a dissenting mind. Now people have a complete trust in me, so I hope I disappoint them, so they won't trust me anymore, as I like to work with people I have to fight against.*

—Jean-Luc Godard, from *Two in the Wave*

# Salò

We are not to be spared.
Some things are too delicious not to be killed.
An orange.
If color is an artist's beloved, it is more so if opposed, or
                                                     juxtaposed—
You must not exist. Your importance
is too important. It led you here.
A vigilante has no choice, he was born that way,
his victim robs him of a good life.
This boy you shot sits on the chair
in your room, smiling.
Your beautiful excrement goes down the drain.
All our paintings paint us into still life.

If you had been spared,
it never would have happened.
You know what *it* is.
Red drapes shut on the new window
as if shopping were a sin.
It is. Everything is a sin. Else why
would you have to pay for it?
(Today we're shopping for young boys and girls.)
The friend whose company you so enjoyed
stopped calling; only years later
did you find out she had died—many, many years later.
You think of flowers
and it's winter.

We are spared in the end
from being spared.
That's what they say—that to suffer
is to live. But many suffer
who are dead, and what saves them is not
knowing it. They who are saved
will never be spared.

In Salò, suffering
is a fascist, an art deco room
furnished as a sumptuous dream.
The chocolate and candied fruit they are eating

at a table set for royalty
are turds of shit. We are not spared
from seeing it as shit, tasting it served in gleaming
bowls of silver. We are
gagging on chocolate and candied fruit.

Perhaps one was worthy as a person and a writer.
But who was to know?
We are spared from knowing we are good.
We killed. We tortured.
We are eating shit
handsomely arranged, straight from the storehouse.
It is brown, it is green, it is well preserved.
We are spared from not knowing what it is,
in Salò. No one says a word.

If you were to tell me I was
happy, I would believe you.
Because trust and happiness are patriotic.
We eat what is on our plates.
We are eaten in deco bliss.

I have never forgotten to be grateful
for the red wheelbarrow and the cold plums.
Everyone's house is freshly painted and cleaned,
everyone has a decent presence on Facebook.
Everyone is edible.
Perhaps this should be a villanelle.
Everyone is spared.
Pasolini was murdered.

# L'Argent

In parts of the Metropolis
they lock up their bad shadow not
in slums but in prisons.
Where they torture it until
it is criminal, an organism
chewing on its own brain.
Later, in some human shape,
released from solitary
it murders a whole family of them, which
is what it takes; then
turns himself in, saying,
as everyone sighs with relief,
I killed for money, I killed in vain.

But only a few are here watching
in the dark theater,
the rest are on film, passing
the rest of the bad money.
The shopkeeper paid off, the student
assured by his mother
that his little crimes will
be covered if he keeps them from
his father, in whose preoccupied office
the story began when the boy
came asking for more money in order to
keep whistling on his motorbike across
the city. Because
there is no whisper of a voice
to lift his shame and
its noise. What we hear is traffic. The lens
focuses on floors, cars, corridors,
hands exchanging money,
to stop, finally, at the terrifying
sounds behind a closed door.

These bills are all over the city,
says the well-dressed woman
to her nameless husband
as they lock up the day's
register, cameras, frames,
the honking street in the window,
the dusty light of one thing polishing
the other's silence.

While the murderer, escaped, is
hidden by a well-to-do angel. And then?
Who can vouch for the flesh of angels—
Nothing is graphic,
              nothing is explicit,
what we see is objective . . . an ax
in the shadow, then
traces of red, in a white sink.

# Mishima

*the writer plots his ritual suicide: directed by Schrader*

Mishima has cut himself in half.
His right side bleeds
Brilliantly colored stories,
His black-and-white side
Plans his demise.
Blue sky, chartreuse fields, red
And orange pavilions—
There can't be any peace
In such vibrant colors.
A man who is cut in half and
Can't bleed should be carried
To a pleasant afternoon in the West
To await his burial
In a French or English garden.
A mix of light. A soft Monet.
Mishima is too crimson for that.
Too black-and-white.
Too double-edged.
Who would have him?
He least of all. And Schrader
Has trouble arranging gray
Restful days, despite the
Old brush paintings . . . Even Kurosawa
Deals in porcelain blues and yellows.
Perhaps times have changed.
At any rate Mishima
Has downright cut himself in half
And there is no blood on the scene.
Though one can imagine paint.
Fresh lights upon yin and yang:
To murder and to mourn the victim at once,
To love and to feel nothing at once,
Leaves the world as it was,
Prehistoric, clean.
A uniform helps.
His suicide had the authority
Of style, crisp and sure.
He did it on the balcony,
For an audience deftly trapped outside.
Immediately, the sky was blue as ice.

# Breathless
   a semi-cento with lines from the film

A black-and-white film
reverts to ash.

*No, it's life.*
*Informers inform,*
*burglers burgle,*
*murderers murder,*
*lovers love.*

*It's too late to be scared now.*
What a sunny day in black and white.

All thoughts out of their cages. Crisp. Crisp.

*It's sad, having to go to sleep;*
*you're forced to part.*

*We say "sleeping together"*
*but it isn't true.*

*I knew that.*
*When we talked I talked*
*about me, you talked about you*
*. . . we should have talked.*

*On the contrary,*
*there's no such*
*thing as being unlucky in love.*

Here we all are, the same colorless. Crisp.

*Still, all things said, it's lovely*
*to be blowing smoke into cool,*
*nonchalant air.*

Yes. It's too late to be scared now.

# Childhood
### after seeing Bresson's four films about imprisonment

upon which everything depends—
why I cuddle up with my lima beans
or inhale a tomato—why
I found you, or you found
me, without thinking, why water
spilled diamonds for us, while others only drank it.

Why I and thou.

Why children signing up to be killers
can't settle down in my dreams

while you think I'm exaggerating again,
and say something about money instead.

A bomb has fallen in the middle
of our living room and no one noticed.
They were tweeting, like birds.
They were posting, unlike the mailman.
They were moving icons around, forgetting
us.

It tarnished everything they saw—
the meaning of our breath, the dust they now smell in
the air and run for the mountains
and build their rebellious huts and leave us
and join up and kill.

*While in your world,*
*they have never done this.*

And so we are left with our childhoods
determining the tides and the eclipse, determining
what you will say to me next.

## *good evening, mr. wallenberg*
### a semi-cento with film titles

dark blue world, earth,
east, west, europa, europa,
where is the friend's house?      says kierostami on a different continent

someone else's america.      where am I?

germany, pale mother.
I was nineteen, pandora's box      opened, I saw
the nasty girl, the bitter tears of petra von kant,
the lost honor of katerina blum—      I was only a child

run, lola, run.
the murderers are among us,      they always are
stalingrad, kadosh!,
eternity and a day.

I was nineteen,      but mother was absent
germany, pale mother,      you were not my mother
heart of glass. good evening
mr. wallenberg.

# Dear pale blue film
### after the 1960 Russian-language version of War and Peace

as if we were already in heaven
wanting only to be human,

to see life through a pearl like
Natasha who moves among birches

and tired oaks suddenly gone lush
with spring. Such killing in soft

pasture blue—killing men, killing
wolf, his eyes curious, his hunger

dying—they remember Natasha
swearing she'd fly into the full

moon's arms—now uniformed
men run feverishly into the arc

of blood of which her French tutors
never told *the little duchess*—but

see her folkdance the soul of old
Russia! as if taught, how she claims

to have lived here before, just
as she will in the future!—so dear to

mother and uncle and the rosy peasants
enchanted—*ah, the fine little lady*

in aqua-blue light—that elsewhere
embraces the dead and dying,

peons and lords all, in the field's
equivalence. *A splendid death* says

the man still on his feet, watching,
through blood-spill, Andrei, whose

voiceover praises the sudden quiet,
the sky opening to him, the magnificence

of death, after all the noise. *It is all
gone, not only War—all—and so this*

*was heaven. It was not what we thought,
but it* was—and they shot it, adds

Tolstoy, straight through its pearl blue
heart, and wrapped it in gauze and mist—

and I with my leaky bucket of blue
beneath a whirl of white-blossoming

trees, a budding so fast, we'll be
forced to dance! Listen to Natasha

even now, beneath the same old
moon. So much has happened

in the gentle field, friend against
friend—*It's madness,* says noble

Pierre, having just shot a man
in a duel, as he stumbles through

thick snow—*everyone is mad!,
everyone has madness in him!*—which

Sergei the director enchants
in a pastel film so forgiving, we get

to live and die in it, just for agreeing
to the holiness he's made of our

mad lives—a wolf dogged down
and tied to a horse, the future

gone cold in his eyes. Poor *Natasha*
was Part II. In Part I

the soldiers get it. Minutes before,
they were singing, led by a clown

marching as the sun is innocent—
as death is to Andrei, listening . . .

*When do we learn,* say the birches in
the soft distance. *When do we learn,*

says his face, hushed in a blue pearl.

# We Are Starlets

*You'll be surprised at how easy you'll find it to like us once you begin.*
—Catch-22

We are cute.
We are ubiquitous.
We are in your cereal.
We are in your serial.
We are in your daughters.
We are in your pantry.
Our teeth are even.
Our smiles ubiquitous.
We are not political.
We are cute.
We don't cook.
We are Jennifers.
We are the name of the year.
We are mirrors.
We are cereal.
We are serial.
We are whole foods.
We are red carpets.
We are the daughters in your sons yes.
We are after you.
We love on a dime.
We are not political.
We are cute.
Our lips sweat cool.
We have cool buns and fresh breast implants.
We are red carpets.
We are pink skin.
We are many, many, many.
We will come after you.
We are sugar to your daughters.
Our cheeks are buns and we open our lips.
We are whole foods.
We are sugared cereals.
We are sugared serials.
We are straight shiny hair in your mirrors.
We love on a dime.

We are on your screens.
We are silver spoons in your mouths.
We are lipstick.
We are coming after you.
We are sugar substitute.
We don't cook.

# The Hours Are Sad

    The hours are sad. We don't know why. We are not afraid of dying but of death. Of both. But we never told the hours.
    We don't understand how the hours can be sad. Nothing but numbers and arms. A face.
    The winds blow around the hours. We don't understand why the winds are angry. Nothing but air and some front chasing. Nothing but trees shattering glass.

    We don't understand why the hours are not angry, only sad, in the midst of the winds shattering trees.
    Perhaps they are tired.
    Nothing but numbers and a round face.
    Ticking surrounds the hours, not at all like a heartbeat. An alien ticking, un-altering, predictable. It says nothing.
        Still, the hours are sad.

# "The tunnel at the end of the light"
*Chinatown* screenwriter Robert Towne on Polanski's original ending

Sometimes
endings are bloodier
without
blood. But what do I know.
We're talking Polanski's answer to
Manson, to the Holocaust,
to the rich wanting to buy

the future.
And dolls. Mother and
daughter
so pretty you could sit them
up
on a bed. You could
rape them both, call them both
daughter, two for one.

Hera was both sister and wife,
and Zeus was all man. Oh yes, and swan.
Ask anything red—it makes
no distinction. Red lords it
over
black-and-white, disdains
yellow,

sepia. And Zeus
repainted Hera
daily.
Sister. Wife. Their gowns flowing

sheer across the mount.
How long
must I stay in this movie,
they asked,
too late,
puking beauty.

# Litany with lines from Paradjanov and Bresson

*An artist creates not by adding but by taking away.*
*We worked to find ourselves in each other.*

We took away the gloss and left the shine.
We took away knowing, we didn't know.
We took away words, the usual words.
We took away acting, we stopped pretending.
We took away pleasing, we loved autonomy.
We took away happiness, we loved too much.
We took away fact, we loved reality.
We took away gold for the sake of hunger.
We removed the children, to see how it felt.
We took away land and dancing horses.
We took away notions of beforelife and afterlife.

*One creates not by adding but by taking away.*

We took away heart, and matter, and notions of beauty
    notions of clothes
        of nakedness
        of effervescence
        of blockbuster baubles
        of the chase
        of piety.
We took away clarity.

*We worked to find ourselves in each other.*

We took away the best and newest equipment.
We took away comfort
                the blights of comfort,
              disease of perfection.
We took away our own health and longevity,
                      and expedience.

*An artist.—Not by adding but by taking away.*

# *The Russian Ark*
### for the only film ever made in one glorious take

1. The Present

Listen . . . don't you ever envy the possible?
    the music no one will ever again
compose, for an empire that will never again
    be?

Doesn't the music still hover? In this gallery
of galleries, this legendary hall lined with
sculptures casual as park benches. Can we still travel
back to that sumptuous century and
    dance?

And you, a love child
    of that billowing ballroom
  among how many hundreds
    still turning and turning and never seeing—my God, is this
the past with its lights—
              no, the most opulent party in history with
plates of solid gold and an orchestra of—
    millions and millions . . . of lights . . . and wigs
        and—as you turn—the unexpected

      shadow a portrait makes—as you glimpse into
a side gallery (keep following our ghostly "guide")—
      a portrait of a man who never knew himself
    as possibly exuberant, brilliant—a costume, really, paint,
      but a costume for a moment awakened
                            but turn
      and in the great hall's windows—

        winter like a frozen diorama,
    a blue diorama of    what        time?

not in *here*, darlings, please don't touch your hearts,
don't feign melancholia—please return to your positions, it is 18 ought ought—

>                    and outside, the snow-blue world like a frozen
>            painting—
>    we are in the Winter Palace, of course—

2. The Past

    Were you good or evil?
    Sweet as apples hung from the sun?
    Bright as dark is bright, as dark goes bright in moments given
       the glory of candles and embers, enchanting earrings, silks stitched for posterity
  or love, the prevailing winds beribboned, frilled,
        and you receiving your deep bows, protected (you're everywhere)
            mournful for some hope
you must have been born with, after all, in some gilded ambience, born
        like a fresh fauna, or a newborn zebra scrambling to stand up—
            is it possible?       Follow and follow
              the *guide*, hush.

  Were you *natural*?
  Were you not the way we raised you
      with our gifted lies?
Just when did you exist? Can you be identified?
    Do you feel taller now, woven in among the dancers
        in such privileged times? (The rest
are peasants in awe, on the periphery.) Can't you feel it coming to an end,
            after all? What did you do with the bowlful
        of red petals, where's your head full of music?

3. The Future

It was all in the sleeves,
the embroidered daisies or posies. In the bare breasts
    faintly damasked, in skirts blooming from waists so pinched
they gave on well-fed roses, or peaches
       dancing. Paintings everywhere . . .
satins' words like kisses in chandeliered air, the sons and daughters
      of monarchs like portly butterflies—*here*, Anastasia, just where you turn

        and nod, flushed
    among bourgeois husbands fleshy with
          wives rosier than the wives of Babbitts. The lights!
              Bursting ladies in besilvered gowns, we pray you be preserved
        in our symphonies for the ages—    Baroquely
            out of reach, as you now must finally
leave the grand ballroom, and we with you,
              as if sated,

pouring out with you down the grandest and widest stairway
        in history
            how elegant and gossipy you are—
      down, down, bejeweled, bare-shouldered, pink and protected ladies,
        down        down the grand stairway
              down down into our
                      ether.

# SPACE

*... because everything has a place, a place far away from reality.*
—Bela Tarr

*The film is the world.*
—Robert Bresson

# That Which Gives Us Life

Read Tranströmer, or see Bergman:
Sweden is dark in winter, dark and mortal.
Herzog travels through scrubby vistas.
My friend Fellini is on a beach with a nutcake
who wants him, or anyone, inside her. She is
a population of one. Waving from shore.
Makhmalbaf focuses on a pastel city,
a mountain spread with fresh-dyed carpets.
The flowers in the fields paint everything
and cameras dry the paint to a shine.
But I live on the plains of Deadfield
on which humans are rarely seen, or
simply resemble the houses, their windows
looking out on each other. Life is
peaceful here, I live mine in subtitled
settings more beautiful than the world.
Outside, I stand looking at the cosmos, wondering
if anyone has heard of it. Something moves,
someone in a car is leaving, how nice,
      though he won't get too far.
It's a long trip from one person to another.

# "Hitchcock loved silence"

Hung a noose on it, joyfully.
Let the birds choke at it, hah.
Let the shower run through it like love
after death, washing away the blood.
Let the fear come suddenly
like a hand on your mouth
from behind.

We hope you have a pleasant fright.

Let the woman in the gray suit be
two. Let the enchanted man
run after her because mystery can
fill an empty room. Let him teeter
above the world, no focus yet. No one there.
No music. Not a whisper.

He coveted clarity. A man looking out
a window seeing clearly defined buildings,
clearly delineated murder—there is an elegance to
being alone with it, a smooth chill hushing
the mind's noise.

A camera follows the man's mind,
who knows less than we do.
(*They pay to be scared,* says Hitchcock with a wink.)
The man can't move. He is crippled.
Yet the world looks rosy. His wife
is in full bloom. She is blonde.

*

It's in silence
that we hear spirits breathing,
some of them evil, others
simply the world reawakening.
Perhaps hoping again.

It never stops turning, the warmed earth,
and in the first pale greening
its variousness breathes, ancient slopes
and human structures rise from
the first primordial mists and
Hitchcock hears birds—

In silence, spirits breathe, even the bad ones
that thrill us with the incomprehensible
looks in their eyes, their axes and knives.
Even the ones with the guns
we used to play with.

But sometimes it's just the earth
reawakening. In silence you can hear it
opening its eyes, listening, stretching its limbs,
as the damp light caresses
the smallest of us with promise, and it's all
audible. It's the silence around us we love,
into which we pour all our noise,

our boom boxes, our bombs, our engines, our flashy
arcades, our gunfire and screams
and sometimes the old mother screams back
and we stop—and listen for the avalanche,
the ground crumbling, tsunamis
advancing, ice melting with a sadness
never before heard
and everything is heard in space, and in time,

well, perhaps not in time, but always in our
vulnerable space.

Hitchcock loved silence.
We too have our reasons.

In silence
your own movie
unfolds

and you stop talking.
It is always your own life and light
and shadows that startle you
most. Your own primordial beginnings, when
childhood has nothing to do with smallness
and all gifts are gifts of time.

# Gabbeh

A painting travels, the soul
of the eye floats in cool water,
the eye is blind,

is life, says the old man.
Color is love, says the girl
to the old woman in herself.

Blue, unlike sky, unlike water,
bluer than poetry, brighter
than the flower from which it comes—
   carpet blue.

              Still you paint,
reaching into the field,
into the bouquet in your hand,
the color in a vat.
              You weave in
the daily losses of yourself, you
as you were, waiting, you
as you were, being told to wait,
you as you were, hoping.

        He saw you weaving,
the caller on the mountain, but
he would not let you go.
              The call of love
is curious, and sometimes
           black.
Blue, pink, orange, the children
wear clothes the color of children,
of petals. Blue
           so thick it blinds
the orange, yellow
hallowing blue, green oceans
of grass, love
           is a paintbrush, is

dipping your hands up to your wrists
in the paint you live in,
           orange, green,
in a sea of grass by the tree, in memory,
        as the old one
will tell you:

When someone dies, we cut
a branch.
      When someone calls, we turn
our eyes toward the tip of the mountain.
        When someone falls from a cliff,
we weave black into the carpet.
           When someone shoots us, we
don't disappear,
    we paint the story
on our gabbeh rinsed in the stream,
        a story
yellower than sunlight, a hundred rugs
  are drying on the mountain.
      This one still floats
a man and a woman on a horse
      in clear water
    washing our gabbeh.

# In the Dark

The light is low.
Either the world or my eyes
failing. Color dims.
What is the body if not memory
contorting, wanting to be blown away?
Living is remembering.
Weakness travels
from heart to lungs
to eyes, and finally to hearing
I love you, I love you, I love you,
like a distant carillon
ever more distant.
They are not violins, they are bells.
Still, it is no longer fashionable
to write of love this way,
and neither was he fashionable,
Pasolini, even while leaving them
           all behind.
That is the fate of the maker.
As for others, their fate is
      yet to be made.

# Faint

This space is holy. This almost air contains a single
essence that floats as many, an odorless perfume—

and if you are holy too, it is left entirely to you
to develop even a single olfactory cell in which

everything manifests as your own breath and
death, the odor of your monologue—the faint odor

of your as yet un-costumed with flesh self,
mingled with the sweet and sour rot of old age

fermenting, which does add oomph to the aromatic
soup of the whole—we taste of each other at all times.

This is and has to be the air we breathe in—this *ours*
developing in an ever more populated space—

and without disdain, or else we'll suffocate, because
what fills in the distance between us is not just

a landscape of snow and ice to keep our pungency
fresh, but rather what we exhale—or jab out

at each other—miles-long missiles of suspicious
stink, like all creatures who protect themselves

with skunk but often can't intuit just who or where
the enemy is, while through all this cod-livering

angels and marigolds and other fragrances drift,
taking up no weight at all, their pleasant perfume

perhaps too alien to matter, too un-there
or anesthetized, or neutralized, or ostracized.

Sometimes I feel faint as if still unborn, unemerged
from the sacred sunlight and leaves, perhaps hoping

to emit, as I'm finally being born, a benign or
else triumphant but still breathable air and,

in growing, grow some hefty thorns in readiness
against the almighty nostrils of the gods.

# To a Child

Yellow birds sing.
They need you to picture a world
in which yellow birds sing.
They need you to pick cherries
off a tree, to reach on tiptoe.
They need you to seduce the sun
out of hiding, this cool day.
One, two, eleven, seven—
to swing high on a swing.
Most of all, they
need you to sing.

# The sets are awash with our leaving

old pearl necklaces, broken rings, dresses
still perfumed and dusted, fine
face powders, brass cufflinks, ascot
ties and pocket watches, well-traveled
shoes, leather and skin, loin
cloths, togas, marble houses and
stick shacks, straw mats, chipped statues
sketched onto canvases, women
burnt alive, smoke rising like prayer, in
the air, in great tempera paintings, yellowed
sheets of music, pyramids still rising
and crumbling, rock by rock, raw skin
against orange sunsets, rainmakers,
snake dancers, blue spirits, green lizards,
great ferns among skyscrapers,
dinosaurs in coffee shops, their
bones clean as pearls, Venus rising
out of half-chimneys, stone
saints fallen out of books and
books bedded down in computers,
all, all, piled high, lucent and trans-
lucent, or sheerly solid, ours to walk
through, battlefields and nurseries, and all
we have to do is sort them out
somehow, organize them, make certain
that earth is properly thanked and
passed on. To whom one gives
what. How to love.

# On Landscape

*What kind of sky would you like?*
—Martin Scorcese, speaking about the digital revolution

The sky is all we have of landscape.
Each day we journey into our hearts
looking for rivers and mountains
straight out of the movies,
a stand of trees and a barn,
a wooden bridge over a creek,
stormy seascapes, devil in the waves.
What do we think this is?
The nineteenth century? No, but
let it be just one potato field, and
a worn-out old woman in rags
looking out into creation. And
an old dog barking, unseen. We know
that somewhere in creation God planted
dogs, like seeds, to grow our notions
of loneliness (in the face of so much
landscape, fields beyond fields, skies
almost unnoticed).           When airplanes
loaded with bombs came our way—
funny how people relieve themselves—
still we had landscapes, and seascapes,
and, on the borders, cityscapes like magic
circuses, cotton candy and sky rises.

Perhaps I'm writing this from the future
while strolling through the remains.

This month I became a poet.
No, it is true.
I had nothing to lose.

The rape of the world left so much
unused, in the landscape devoid of landscape.
Was it Michelangelo or Bresson who first said one
creates not by adding but by taking away?

The landscape is chipping away, an uninvited
sculptor digging for some essence—
as if he wants it to loom, a vision beyond all
visions.

But here now comes a scattering
of summer clouds, just above the trees—
yes, there still are a few trees, short
and humble as a dog's yips and just as
man-made—here come a few
cloud-soft clouds, rolling into a blank-blue sky—
refusing someone's idea of perfection,
adding some wind-driven fantasy our way.
And suddenly and all at once, we're back in
the country of the clouds.

Which is what I called the story for children
I wrote in another life.

What delicious blue clouds, the sun,
through a sudden portal, shoots down
long shining rays—this is where
the notion of angels started.
And the notion of gods? The portal
has just shut—the clouds are darkening
from the west, like the painterly side of some
tragedy, though everything is still summer and
flashes of light.

Now the sky is half-empty, half-full
of the radiance we call celestial,

now coming in center stage as
                      landscape—
    a flash and I'm captured
in the last sunburst—

and it's over, along with the
blue we covet.
We are in the country of the clouds,
   children, where everyone
      is iridescent.

## She replied,

This is not about the movies.
This is about us. Ah, I can see
the look on your face. Not
that *poet* is the greatest thing to be.
But knowing who you are is.
We need the movies to tell us
we are poets.

*Amarcord* was. Fellini followed
to the ends of the earth, and
it led him to his hometown.
Don't blame me for loving Fellini.
How can you not love someone who's
so in love with his makers:
*Amarcord. La Dolce Vita.* All of them.
Or Nino Rota for falling in love
with the rhythm that made him dance—
                              *she continued*—I
love the sun for needing me
to shine on. So many bowls of fruit
and landscapes needed Cézanne's brush,
but even more did the paintings,
and he loved them.
                    This is our bible. First
comes *Amarcord*, then Fellini. Not
that magic is so wonderful. But
it needs me. I am the deck of cards
and the wand. I am the mango
dripping down your chin,
else why would you love me?

No—*she replied*—this is not about the movies.
This is about the emptiness that needs
to make one world at a time, the poor cosmos
that needs each star, if only for its light.
This is not about the master
but about the dog, begging.

# We

Not I but the reef of us
alive in the sun.
For I am but that island of light
Emily has seen,
and she, my neighboring light.

Unphotographed multitudes,
perhaps never recorded as one.
We, faces in a choir.
We, faces on fire, then
ashen, fused into eternity.
Can you even imagine
a photo of all of us on earth
       together?
Yet of course it is there.
And we are face and camera both.
And the image has to be taken
       in the heart.

# *Immortal beloved,*
### for the subject of the biopic on Beethoven

turn things around and
it doesn't matter what
your drama attained, what pitch—the end
is more important

grander
a music richer than any
love lost—

no.

So unique a life
so honest and deserving and how difficult
the talented life
but the ending is
more—

no.

There I am in the mirror
in an amber otherworld wide
with music

the longest night
reflecting my lovely legs
dancing, the unkillable—

yes

so many dreams I've lived
and they seemed so real, you
touched one

that foreign element, the not you
sizzling in its own want
cooling—

no.

Nothing ends.

# Touch

after the documentary *Cosmos*, with Neil DeGrasse Tyson

So we won't be here for the disappearance of the stars.

The moon will implode first, earth will go flying asunder,

we ourselves dispersed as stars. O world,

every shred of us distant and beautiful.

Here we sit around the table with our poems,

having forgotten what matter we come from

and where it is going, blithely fragmenting as we speak

words into the starlit unknown, goodbye

and hello merging into a single shine.


Love to you out there, love.

*For a film buff, life's purpose is to reunite in the kingdom of shadows.*
—François Truffaut


*It fades and we see what cinema really is—a pure light.*
—Alexandro Jodorowsky, *The Holy Mountain*

# Acknowledgments

*"L'Argent"* first published in *Spoon River Poetry Review*

*"Mishima"* first published in *Another Chicago Magazine* and *On a Good Day One Discovers Another Poet* (Finishing Line Press, 2009)

*"Ponette"* first published in *On a Good Day One Discovers Another Poet* (Finishing Line Press, 2009)

# About the Author

**Helen Degen Cohen** was born Halina "Halinka" Degenfisz on November 19, 1934, in Grojec, near Warsaw, Poland. During World War II she was kept in hiding by Maria Szumska. Helen and her parents, Joseph Degen and Bluma "Bella" (Dreyer) Degen, eventually settled in Chicago. She graduated from Trinity University and later received an MFA from the University of Illinois at Chicago. She married Arnold Cohen, and they had three children: Richard Scott, Daniel, and Laura. Later she married Donald Memmer, who preceded her in death.

Helen had a long career as a writer and educator. She was an elementary school teacher, taught college classes, and toured the state of Illinois as an Illinois Artist-in-Residence. She cofounded and coedited the *RHINO Poetry Journal*. An acclaimed poet, short-story writer, and novelist, Helen received many awards, most notably a National Endowment for the Arts Fellowship in Poetry, three Illinois Arts Council Literary Awards in fiction and poetry, first prize in the UK-based *Stand* magazine's international short story competition, and the Paladin Award for extraordinary long-term contributions to poetry in Illinois. She also received fellowships to major arts colonies, including Yaddo, MacDowell, and Ragdale.

Helen's earlier poetry collections are *Habry, or The End of Snow* (Puddin'head Press, 2009) and the chapbooks *On a Good Day One Discovers Another Poet* (Finishing Line Press, 2009) and *Neruda Nights* (nominated for a Pushcart Prize; Finishing Line Press, 2012). She died in 2015, shortly after facilitating the November session of her beloved Rhino Poetry Forum, a peer workshop for poets.

## About Helen's Legacy

Ralph Hamilton, lead editor of *RHINO*, performed a labor of love by compiling and reordering *My Life on Film* from a sprawling manuscript Helen had submitted to Glass Lyre Press. Some final work was done by a team of poets/writers/editors who were also close to Helen—Michael Anderson, Ruth Goring, Susanna Lang, and Andrea Witzke Slot—along with Laura Cohen, Helen's daughter. The "Helen legacy team" is dedicated to compiling and publishing the best remaining work of this remarkably gifted and prolific writer.

# Glass Lyre Press

exceptional works to replenish the spirit

Glass Lyre Press is an independent literary publisher interested in technically accomplished, stylistically distinct, and original work. Glass Lyre seeks diverse writers that possess a dynamic aesthetic and an ability to emotionally and intellectually engage a wide audience of readers.

Glass Lyre's vision is to connect the world through language and art. We hope to expand the scope of poetry and short fiction for the general reader through exceptionally well-written books, which evoke emotion, provide insight, and resonate with the human spirit.

Poetry Collections
Poetry Chapbooks
Select Short & Flash Fiction
Anthologies

www.GlassLyrePress.com

www.ingramcontent.com/pod-product-compliance
Lightning Source LLC
Chambersburg PA
CBHW021156080526
44588CB00008B/365